This Heart of Mine

This Heart of Mine

This Heart of Mine

Kaci Diane

This Heart of Mine

Library of Congress Cataloging-in-Publication Data
Diane, Kaci
This Heart of Mine/ Kaci Diane
ISBN: 978-0-9985045-1-3
1. Loss 2. Healing 3. Hope 4.Poetry
5. Inspiration   6. Growth

Printed in the United States of America
Book Design by Jonathan Day and Kaci Diane

To my family and friends.

Contents

This Heart of Mine

This Heart of Mine

This Heart of Mine

Introduction

This Heart of Mine

This Heart of Mine

This heart of mine is not some pretty house for looking at, it has been lived in. Lived in by tenants who had to be evicted. Abandoned by tenants I didn't want to leave.

This heart has been damaged by visitors who have overstayed their welcome; people who should have only been a porch visit that I invited to come inside. Since then...

Walls have been built. Walls have been torn down. Lessons have been learned. New house rules have been applied.

This heart. This home where I reside has been purged, stripped down to the bare essentials. It has been renovated, redecorated, and gone through many foundational changes.

It took a lot of work, but it is now ready to let people in again.

My Synopsis

This is who I am.

A composition of melanin, organs, and finger nails. DNA, heart to hearts, and good old-fashioned beat downs. I am life changing revelations, tear stained pillows on lonely nights. I am moments spent in front of the mirror searching for the girl that sits behind two brown eyes, a nose, and hair that is free to do as it pleases.

I am effortlessly amazing; a woman worthy of adoration. One who is taking classes in humility and compassion on a daily basis; majoring in human understanding with a concentration in the ability to love people genuinely.

I say I'm sorry more than I say you're welcome, but I am teaching myself to ask better questions. "What's wrong with me?" is no longer acceptable. I surround myself with people who not only inspire me but challenge me. I search for the peace that transcends all understanding in mundane day to day activities. I send up Dear God letters on the regular, alternating between adoring fan, cynical critic, and confused observer.

I am constantly familiarizing myself with my own voice and redefining what it means to be beautiful. I am a woman teaching myself how to love myself. I allow others to impact me while at the same time holding my ground. I am a paradoxical paradigm of misunderstandings. I second-guess myself way too much and when people say I am intimidated by my own voice I don't disagree with them. I don't fully understand the depth of my impact.

My heart is too big for me to handle by myself. I have an abundance of love and I look for people to share in my wealth. I have two parents that love each other deeply, yet live in separate houses. I learned early on that despite what romantic comedies have tried to teach me, love is not all you need. It can get you in the car, but it won't drive you to forever.

I love poetry and I love singing. When I sing I feel free. When I write poetry I feel understood. The combination has been healing for me. I never want to stop missing the people I've lost. I never want to forget how their lives changed the way I view mine. I am learning how to love like water, with palms open, allowing people to ebb and flow in and out of my life without taking their absence so personally. I speak my truth. Even when the words don't come out perfectly they are still just as cleansing.

I let go of negative feelings and people: neither have made me any happier. I know that tears don't stop me from smiling and anger is only used to cover up what I am trying to hide. I say everything I need to say in case you are no longer around to hear it; I ask for what I want without fear of the word no.

I am gentle enough to quench thirsts and powerful enough to move mountains. I am patient and persistent at the same time. I know what I want, yet it takes time to see if what I want wants me. A good thing can easily turn into a bad thing if I pursue it too aggressively. I know what is mine will always be mine and what is not mine will always leave a scar. I say "I love you" with my actions long before I say it with words. I never want the recipient to question my sincerity.

I live like water, plotting my course through this world with the knowledge that I am determined enough and forgiving enough to make it where I am meant to be.

Story Time

So this is my story. It's not my whole story, just part of it.
Life is so funny that way, it just keeps on happening.
It's important not to get stuck feeling sorry for yourself.
When storms come through sometimes all you can do is wait it out.
The waiting is what changes people:
waiting for things to return to the way they were,
waiting for people to come back,
waiting for the pain to stop,
waiting for things that may or may not ever happen.
While waiting we learn tactics to adjust to our new reality.
Basically, we learn to cope.
Writing is how I cope.
It's how I heal and adjust and make room for hope.

To All of My Ghosts

Hello. This conversation is one I didn't know I was capable of having. I assumed because all of you are no longer in my life, communicating was not an option. Then I realized that while none of you are physically present, all of you are still with me everywhere I go. I have been carrying you and you all are heavy. Many times, the sheer weight of my past exhausts me, which is terrifying because I am still so very young.

I have been contemplating how to move forward in my life while traveling with such heavy luggage. This is why I have decided to confront you all head on. I don't expect you to leave me alone. You have made it quite clear that you are not going anywhere, so what I need you to do is walk. You may travel beside me, but not on top of me. I need to be able to function. I need to stay in the present. I need to value every moment. I need to not be afraid to love people.

I think this is a reasonable compromise. I will not try to get rid of you and you will not try to destroy me. After all, when you were alive there was love shared between us. You were my family, my friends, my teachers, my love. When you were alive I don't believe you would have ever tried to hurt me, so now that you are gone I assume you follow me because you are trying to look after me. It seems over the last couple of years I have been collecting an army of angels. Although I didn't recognize you at first, angels can be very scary if they don't introduce themselves -- if they don't tell you what their intentions are.

Learning how to put you down has allowed me to learn how to let go of people who haven't died. They are harder to set free, because when people are alive a little piece of you is always waiting for them to come back. In a way, they are ghosts of mine too. People don't have to be dead to haunt you. And being haunted doesn't have be a scary thing. I look at you, all of my ghosts, and I see all the things I have survived. I see all the love I have encountered in my lifetime. It amazes me, because I am still so very young.

5

It's Unfortunate

It's unfortunate you know,
that these are the experiences that have shaped me;
and that writing is how I deal with those experiences;
and that I desire to make a living writing;
thus, making me way more susceptible to vulnerability than those
who have other professions.
My life would be much more private if I could deal with things
through yoga or dancing or talking.
I do those things too.
Those things bring a lot of clarity,
but honestly they don't take away my desire to write.
They make the words flow faster,
with more depth,
and with a sharpened articulation.
The hardest part,
is sharing my words with people who kind of know me
or who used to know me
or who only know me in a certain environment.
It's easier to be vulnerable with best friends.
They have already committed to loving you.
You know there is nothing you can say to change that.
It's easiest to be vulnerable with strangers.
They don't judge.
Rather, their judgement doesn't mean as much;
the threat of their disapproval is not as daunting.
Whatever category of people you find yourself in I want you to know
how much writing has helped me.
It has given me no choice but to face myself, and by facing myself
I have learned how to adjust, how to grow, how to heal.
For many years I have kept the bulk of my writing to myself,
but on my 26th birthday I wept.
I didn't shed tears.
Salt water droplets did not glisten on my cheeks,
there was nothing flowery about what my soul was trying to tell me.
It had been telling me the same thing for years,

that these words are not just for me.
It was that day I decided to listen.
To really listen.
The kind where you put your money where your mouth is.
I don't know who my words are meant to touch.
What I do know is that no matter how uncomfortable I feel...
I. Did. My. Part.
I heard and obeyed.
If nothing else I say resonates with you, take this: if your soul is
telling you to do something I encourage you to listen. To really, really
put your money where your mouth is -- listen.

Rejection

We Remember

we remember moments
we remember feelings
we remember brief interactions and glimpses of eye contact
we remember touches
skin against skin
fingers that graze fingers
just enough
too much and our sensors would overload
we remember sensations
vivid heartbeats
we remember sound fragments
snapshots of bonfires
shoulders barely meeting
stolen glances across crowded areas
we remember smiles
half smiles
hidden smiles
we remember comfort
we remember jealousy
we remember disappointment
we remember
we remember
we remember
easily misinterpreted moments

If You Don't Want to Hurt Me

If you don't want to hurt me, then don't touch me.
Don't cup the back of my head with one hand and wrap the other around the small of my back.
Don't pull me towards you.
Don't drench me in your kindness.
Don't let me go home smelling like you.

If you don't want to hurt me, then don't stand so close to me.
Don't kiss my wounds with your tongue if you have no intention of kissing my lips.
Don't hold me like a lover if you have no intention of loving me.
Don't look at me with those eyes, and expect me to look away.
Don't make me fall in love with you, then say that you don't love me too.

If you don't want to hurt me, then don't hold my gaze for too long.
Don't tell me you are just being nice.
Don't tell me that you treat all girls like this.
Don't tell me that I'm overreacting.
Don't tell me that I'm not as special as you make me feel.

If you don't want to hurt me, then don't smile at me when I enter a room.
Don't buy me little gifts.
Don't tell me I deserve better.
Don't make me feel excited and terrified at the same time.
Don't make me feel like knowing you is spoiling myself and walking away is self-deprivation.

If you do not want to hurt me, then know what you want. If it's not me, then...
Don't be afraid to walk away.
Don't reply to my messages.
Don't return my phone calls.
Don't, just don't.

Too Much

he said:
you are too much fire
not enough burn cream
too much get it yourself
not enough cater to you
too much "i got this"
not enough "what do you think"
too much "this conversation is over"
not enough "how did we get here"
too much sass
not enough submission
too much "I'm awesome"
not enough "you're awesome too"
he said. he said. he said
all of these things before saying goodbye.
i am:
too much let it go
not enough stick it out
too much baggage
not enough roller bags
too much self-sabotage
not enough overcome insecurities
too much transition
not enough stability
too much fear of commitment
not enough do you really want to die alone
too much standing in your own way
not enough letting people in
too much lone wolf
not enough ride or die
too much bird
not enough tree
too much acceptance of the idea of dying young
not enough acceptance of the idea of growing old
too much ready for rejection
not enough praying for acceptance

too much sarcastic comebacks
not enough vulnerable conversations
too much "well fine"
not enough "please stay"
too much "I'm better off without you"
not enough "I no longer want to live this way"
too much "I'm OK"
not enough "I need help"
too much "be brave"
not enough "I'm scared"
too much "nothing in my life is permanent"
not enough "this is what I'm working to keep"
too much "but people leave"
not enough "but love them anyway"
too much waiting for an instant spark
not enough fanning the flames
too much everyday should be a grand adventure
not enough realistic expectations
too much hopping around
not enough standing still
too much "this is boring"
not enough "but it's worth it"
too much hoping my next stop will be better
not enough this stop is pretty great
too much self-preservation
not enough putting myself out there
too much broken relationships
not enough reconciliation
i am. i am. i am
i really am sorry.

Memorizing

Maybe I was wrong for memorizing the plains of your face; the arch of your eyebrows; the wetness in your eyes after you blink; the little stubble of hair you had when you tried to grow a mustache. It's still funny.

And the way you laughed, not an angry laugh but a "stop teasing" laugh. You were so cute. This funny-looking boy that had my heart doing somersaults. What did you do to me? We were happy. But now I don't even know what I am. I don't feel normal. It doesn't feel good, but I can't say it's bad.

I mean, I think I was in love with you. Who really knows what that means, though. Seems like everyone has their own personal definition. I didn't get a chance to finish writing mine. When you smiled, oh, your smile made me smile. And when I was crying you had your own way of making me forget why I was sad.

Who's going to make me forget now? I will never forget this feeling. Death waits by my bedside taunting me. I'm scared, but who can I call? You were my best friend. It's been over a year and you are still my best friend. Nobody even compares to you.

Sometimes I reflect on all the things I did wrong, all the ways I hurt you. How I challenged your pride, how I questioned everything. I don't even know why you loved me. I still don't understand how anybody could love someone like me. I wouldn't even let myself love you back.

My fear kept you at arm's length and now I would give anything to hold you. I'm sorry. I'm sorry it took losing you to find you. I'm sorry it took losing you to find me. And it pains me to say this, but your death was the best thing to happen to me. It made me open my eyes. It made suffering real and forgiveness possible.

I was not the only one who was hurting. Hand guns revolving around your head, two fingers on the trigger to make sure it clicks and you're done, we're done, you're over. It's been some time now and I'm just starting to get over it. I'm starting to forgive myself. I wasn't meant to be the one that saves you. I was meant to be the one that sees you, that loves you.

You were meant to show me that I need to open my eyes.

Haunted

I'm not allowed to be mad at you. You were in a fight against a disease and you lost. That's how they told me to think about it -- as a disease. I understand to some extent, but to another, I don't.

That's not the point, I guess. You really did want to get better. You told me you wanted to get better for us. For you and for me so that one day we could provide the childhood your father never provided for you. I had such high hopes. Such vivid dreams about our future.

I'm trying really hard not to be mad. I'm trying really hard not to let the sorrow break me. We were supposed to… I can't even finish the sentence. It's too cliché. Not everyone gets the privilege of growing old with the one they love. Who was I to think I'd be so lucky?

It's okay. Really, I'll be okay. I can forgive you for leaving me. Maybe not today, but eventually.

Rest well, okay?

P.S. Remember, that no matter how disappointed I am, that doesn't stop me from loving you. I miss you. I will forgive you. And I will do my best not to be haunted by you.

Death

The Breaking

It's the pulling apart and the breaking
the pulling apart and the breaking.
The shifting of existence.
The love; the loss.
The loss of love.
The shattered reality.
The dashing hope.
The tears; the anger.
The overwhelming misery of loneliness.
But mainly, it's the pulling apart and the breaking.
The pulling apart and the breaking
going from two back to one again.

Not Ready for Goodbye

What if I'm not ready for goodbye?
Will you still leave?
Would you say goodbye anyway?
If I say hello over and over again could that negate your one goodbye?
What if I don't hear you ask to be excused from my life?
What if I hear you but don't acknowledge your request?
What if I hear you and plainly state that you are not excused?
That you do not have my blessing to leave.
Will you still leave?
What if I cry?
What if I bang my fists on the table, pull at my hair,
scream as loud as I can?
Will you still leave?
What if I just beg quietly and earnestly?
What if I get on my knees?
What if I grovel at your feet?
Will you step over me towards the door or will you stoop down and
help me up?
Will you gather me in your arms?
Will you help me to bed and comfort me until I fall asleep?
Will you pack quietly?
Will you leave in the night?
Will I awake to find a note filled with apologies?
Or will it have just one sentence that states:
I love you, but I have to go.

Words

Words are really hard for me today.
Words.
I just need words.
I need some kind of method
to express to you the longings of my thoughts.
I just need words.
To express to you the agonizing pull working with gravity to collapse
my fragile heart.
I need his words.
Not to hear him say goodbye one last time.
Not for them to soothe me as I cry.
I need his words to whisper dialect into my subconscious.
Remind me how to form sentences.
What are phrases?
What are questions?
Where lies truth?
I need words.
It wasn't until he left that I was left speechless.
It wasn't until he left that I saw how I took words for granted.
In the end, all I have are these words.
Memories ingrained on paper;
etched into the hearts of people, whose lives I've grazed.
I need words.
Words.
That is all that I need.

Questions for the Dead

Is it possible that the dead walk among us?
Do they sit on our couches as we sit at the desk?
Do they submerge themselves into our dreams?
Kiss our foreheads when we cry?
Stroke our hair when we are sick?
Do they reach for us as we walk through them?
Try to make eye contact when we stare in the mirror, using our own
eyes as windows to their souls?
Do they love us through the grave?
Miss us too much to watch over us from a place as far away as
heaven?
Do they fear for our safety to the extent they prefer to accompany us as
we walk among the living?
Was it balance that stopped me from falling down the stairs, or
someone else?
Do the dead delight in their ability to make the strongest of the living
cry, or do they mourn solely because we are mourning?
If heaven exists what does it look like?
Is floating among the living an option?
Could the remorseful be shown mercy in hell?
Is it possible to fully grasp the concept of eternity?
Would I be okay if after life was just death?
If heaven and hell were ploys God came up with to make the living
behave.
If no matter how we lived, we all ended up the same. Gone.
Would that change the way I lived?
That would mean that the spirits that look over us, and walk among us
are just figments of our imagination.
The mind's way of making us feel protected
when all we have is who we have among us.
Once our bones wither away,
would I be okay with simply being a memory?

Spanish Proverb

"If the sky falls, hold up your hands."

When the sky begins to fall, instinctively, we hold up our hands.
We try to protect ourselves.
We try to push it back up.
We seek help.
We seek security in our strength.
We soon realize we are not strong enough.
We soon realize we cannot stop the sky from falling.
We surrender.
We hold up hands with fingers clutched around white flags.
We wave them frantically.
We cry out in desperation.
We get angry.
We misdirect our anger.
We blame others.
We blame ourselves.
We blame God.
We wallow in self-pity.
We choke on hatred.
We grow numb to other people's suffering.
We compare grief.
We measure scars to decide who is more worthy of expressing pain.
We feel ungrateful if we lose.
We feel a false sense of satisfaction if we win.
We collapse to our knees.
We begin to accept our helplessness.
We hold up our hands towards the heavens.
We pray.
We pray to a God we used to know.
We want know.
We want understand.
We ask questions.
We ask boldly.
We ask in barely a whisper.
We ask with the shrugging of shoulders and nodding of heads.

We ask with mute voices, too broken to beg for mercy.
When the sky falls, all we can do is hold up our hands.

The Waves

I want to be around people who see the special kind of beauty that comes from survival. The biggest lesson I took from my intensified learning years is that pain doesn't just go away.

Sorrow is an ocean one has to swim in. And no matter how many people you have that love you, you must swim alone.

There will be many days where it feels like you are drowning. You will wonder if this is the way you are going to die. You will look up and not see any shore in any direction, and turning back will not be an option.

The waves will exhaust you and constantly threaten to overpower you. Breathing will be difficult. You will want to give up. Every day you will want to give up.

But if you keep going over time, breathing will get easier. You will learn to pace yourself because grief is not a race. It is not something that ends. It is an ocean you learn to live in.

You learn to manage the waves. You learn to float. And people who float on this ocean of sorrow possess a special kind of beauty -- one that can only be acquired by learning how to manage the waves.

This Heart of Mine

Grief

This Heart of Mine

�֎

In the morning,
when I wake to bruised knuckles and bloody fingers
I can breathe easy
knowing I had the courage to hold on
and the courage to let go.

My youth has misled me.
I was assured years to acquire romance
and decades to acquire wisdom.
However, time made no such promises.

This Heart of Mine

✦

I've grown accustomed to walking by myself.
I couldn't bear the thought of having
interlace their life with mine,
only to peel the memory of their fingers from my hands.

☀

Please know,
that I don't know.
I don't know how to say I need you without coming across as
desperate.
I don't know how to be reserved without coming across as cold.

☀

She is the lone survivor in a personal earthquake.
Others have seen the impact -- light feet carrying a heavy heart.
This ground is always quaking, don't trust the silence.
This steadiness is unnerving, temporary, devastatingly deceitful.
She turns her head and the earth quakes again.
People pause and glance, then move around like the ground is not
breaking beneath them.

You have been waiting for a time that will never come.
You have been waiting for skies that will never rain,
cars that will always run,
and hearts with an infinite number of beats.
But that's not real life.
Rain will always come.
Cars get old, tired, and rusty -- eventually they stop running.
And hearts, hearts stop beating with or without our consent.
We all mourn from time to time,
but the living have an obligation to live.

*

It's been a year since hell broke loose.
People are busy; I have to make appointments to be consoled.
The leaves are browning, crinkling, and slowly
finding their way to the ground.
I am doing the same.

not broken.
overflowing
spilling over
no longer capable of containing self
stop trying to fix; just listen
let overflow
let trickle
let drizzle
let drop
catch as falling
touch gently or not at all

10 years of sadness evaded all because I let one year slip by.
Busy, busy, busy am I.
Here comes year two; still, I have no time to cry.
Years 3, 4, 5 still no time.
6, 7, 8, 9 much of the same.
10. I am at year 10 and when the first leaves fall,
the rain storms begin.
But I plaster on a smile.
I shove it back in, and proceed to a 2nd 10.

✸

I didn't use to think this hard about what it means to be alive.
I used to just live.
My insides are congested with words unsaid,
bear with me as I try to explain.
I'm not used to giving so much of myself to so many people.
You should know that trying to shove my unruly emotions into tidy
3×5 minute poems is equivalent to trying to shove my body into
skinny jeans that are two sizes too small.
No matter how I jiggle my hips and jump up and down
there will always be pieces of me left out.

Insanity

This Heart of Mine

Bursting

I am bursting.
I am explosives on the inside
will somebody give me a night sky.
I am rain clouds and thunderstorms.
I am a death not properly mourned.
I am earthquakes trembling, quivering,
begging to erupt.
I am walls and walls and walls
eager to collapse.
I am fear not allowed to be felt.
I am tears that won't come.
I am a cracking dam that keeps getting patched
sweet Jesus, let me burst!

What Journals Are For

Journals are for the multiple voices the world drives us to create.
It is a safe place for them to speak.
In short, it is insanity unleashed.
Here you will be looked at strange if you try to keep it together.
We will make fun of you.
Spit at you.
Throw feces at your face until you stop pretending you are not like us.
Here we torment the "normal,"
we insult,
poke fun at,
push buttons until deranged;
until homelessness;
until destitute;
until insecure;
until past insecure;
until submerged in it;
until engulfed in it;
until void of cohesive thought;
until dead on the inside;
until anger;
until you push back.
Then we will beat you into submission- until you beat back,
until you run down streets,
lit fingers,
torn hair,
attempting to slit your wrists with spoons,
and drown yourself in puddles.
We will torture you into strength,
then when you are strong we will beat you into weakness.
You will not know what we want and we will not tell you because we
will not know.
We will laugh at you as you become like us.
We will turn on each other;
we are fresh blood-always.

The torturous cycle will never stop.
After a while you won't want it to.
That is when you know you are a part of us.
That is when you know you are using your journal correctly.

Insanity

Well, this is embarrassing.

It seems I have misplaced my mind. Would you be so kind as to help me find it? Oh, there it is. Sanity, right? It's such a slippery thing to hold onto. All oozing and sliding between my fingers. I want to keep it together, but how am I to grasp something that has no true form?

People have told me I won't make it in the real world. That's fine. I don't very much like the real world. I would much rather sit here and go quietly insane.

Truthfully, I don't want to do so quietly. I would much prefer running down the streets of New York weeping openly, but I've noticed that makes people uncomfortable. I saw a homeless woman crying on the sidewalk and was jealous of her. Nobody told her to stop crying. Nobody scolded her for interrupting their comfort.

It is quite embarrassing to be so publicly shattered. Brokenness looks a lot like insanity. Only she didn't care, and maybe I shouldn't either.

It seems it is necessary to break down in order to break out of other people's expectations. The ones that tell us to be hard, to man up, to toughen up, to never let the world see us cry.

Well, I don't want to be hard. 'Cuz I know it will hurt that much more when I am broken again. I am tired of pretending to be stronger than I actually am. It is okay to be weak sometimes. It is okay to break.

Pleading

Dear You,
Tell me:
that I am worthwhile;
that I am sweet;
that I am beautifully imperfect; worthy of adoration;
that I am wonderful;
that it is okay to be broken;
that You will fix me;
that You will love me despite that;
love me in light of that;
love me because of that.
Help me claim the strength of vulnerability.
Help me forgive:
forgive myself,
forgive others.
Help me move on.
Teach me compassion and empathy,
show me through example.
Tell me, that even when it feels like I have nothing left to give
I have so much more than I know.

Everything

this is a poem
this poem is not about you
it's about everything
everything that happens to be happening at one time
but not really
it's about things happening gradually
but not having a safe place to regularly explode
it's about not forcing a smile when you don't feel like smiling
it's about privacy and throwing it out the window and immediately
wanting it back
it's about not knowing when to take action and when to be patient
it's about scalding hot showers in an attempt to tame the rage
it's about screaming to stop you from holding your breath
it's about walking for so long that you are too tired to walk back home
it's about everything and nothing
but mostly everything
this poem is about everything.

Healing

God Has Been Stalking Me

I went to his house this morning and found mental snapshots of me from his perspective. He left them right there in my mind like he wanted me to find them. One was of me in a monastery, kneeling before a monk, rubbing gift-shop prayer beads between my fingers.

Another was of me sitting in a synagogue, staring at the eternal light that hung above a cabinet storing the Old Testament inscribed on scrolls. A third was of me sitting across the street from a beautiful cathedral, too terrified to go inside.

I sat in God's house on a couch that used to smell like me. My hands laid firmly on my knees and I tried to overlook the evidence that God followed me when I ran away from him. Politely, he offered me bread and wine, which I accepted out of habit. He played nice music and I swayed. He spoke directly to me and I listened.

When my visit was over I got up to leave but something stopped me. The other guests maneuvered around me to the door. Some tried to speak to me; to ask me if I was okay. One was kind enough to attempt to wipe the tear that drifted down my check, but I pushed their hand away. The other guests whispered and stared until eventually they all left.

Alone in God's house I fell to my knees as he played the accelerated soundtrack of my life since my baptism. It started out joyful and upbeat. I had almost forgotten what my voice sounds like when it is happy. It was nice to be reminded. I was beginning to remember things I used to do -- little things like smiling, and laughing, and singing, and dancing. I was beginning to remember what happiness felt like.

Slowly the track began to skip and my laughter got choppy, abbreviated, cut short. The CD skipped to the next track and on came a voice I did not recognize. Technically it was my voice, but the words were not my thoughts. The laughter my voice produced was not genuine and, shortly after, nonexistent. The CD skipped to the next track and all I could hear was the sound of a CD player searching for the next song. I had expected silence, but there is a distinct sound that comes with searching. If sounds had feelings it would feel like straining, like agony, like desperation. It would feel like me.

You Love Me

Did I forget to tell you everything sizzles when you touch me?
And still all I pray you do is touch me.
In the quiet I contemplate why you chose me.
I recall the pain of being thrown in the fire.
I recall how flesh smells as it's being ruined.
You ruin me in the best possible way.
You are a torch in an ocean of solitude.
You love me, fire engine red.
You love me smoke cloud grey.
You love me suffocating flames.
You love me burning ember.
You love me to ruins.
You love me to death.
You love me to life.
You love me to resurrection.
You love me again.
You love me all over again.

Grandmother

I look at you and I see the woman I want to be, the woman I could be, the woman I am afraid to be. I don't know if I am strong enough to have faith like yours.

Now, I've seen faith up close -- I see it every time I look into my mother's eyes -- but I have never seen faith this amplified.

At the grave site, you stood before your family and his loved ones and spoke of love, God's love, an incomprehensible love.

You stood, head held high, looked grief in the face, and smiled the most graceful of smiles as you laid your son beside his father.

Grandmother, with a pain this back-breaking, is God the reason you are able to stand so straight?

How to Free Write

Step one.
Place pen on paper
or fingers on keys
and write.
Write through social norms and what is expected of you.
Stop thinking, just write.
Rid yourself of worries, doubts, happiness, sadness, triumphs, failures
and everything in between.
Write it all down.
Say all the things you would never say out loud.
Write like sympathy for others seem pointless.
Leave paper trails of guilty thoughts
no one will be reading this but you.
Write as if time is suspended,
like you have nowhere to go
and no one is waiting for you.
Write until death is no longer scary;
until suicide doesn't make a strong enough statement;
until loneliness doesn't seem scarier than dying.
Write like your life is a never ending prayer
and God will defend your intentions.
Wade through all your b.s. and you will reach your truth.
Just write.
Let your tears flow,
let laughter reverberate in your vocal cords
and anger will evaporate from your spirit.
Keep going.
If you're doing it right
your thoughts will shift to beyond recognition.
You will feel like the person you never knew you wanted to be.
You will be ecstatic and terrified at the same time.
From there, keep writing;
until your mind is void of every synonym for emotion.

Write, until you are empty.
Delightfully exhausted.
Weightless of everything you try so hard to hold on to.
When you reach that point,
when you have nothing left to say
lean back,
place your hands on your lap,
and relax.
There is no step two.

I Know

Here I am again, slipping into depression. I know the rage is a cover-up. I know the sorrow is real. I know the fear, the rejection, and the uncertainty is also real. I know I will be okay. I know that God's got me. I know that this phase is only a test.

I know depression is a disease I have beaten before. I know how to sing after crying. I know how to laugh after falling down. I know how to admit when I need help.

I know that I am young. I know that I am growing. I know that I am never too old to want my mom. I know I feel like work. I know I'm difficult to figure out. I know I sometimes **I** feel like a heavy load. I know that I am worth it. I know I'm more good than bad.

I know that I am blessed. I know that I am grateful. I know that I will always have more to give. I know that love will find me. I know that love takes time. I know that what is mine will not pass me by.

I know that I am beautiful. I know that I am kind. I know that others see it, too. I know that I'll be fine. I know that I will grow. I know that everything will work out. I know that joy is contagious. I know that joy is holy. I know that joy is worth the fight. I know that I've fought before. I know I'll fight again. I know I need to start fighting now.

I know that memory is malleable. I know that understanding is easily manipulated. I know that my reality is shaped by what I choose to believe. I know that "they" are not the problem. I know that I am my solution. I know my happiness is up to me.

I know how to train my brain. I know how to feed it good stuff. I know how to make it nice and strong. I know I don't really know what I'm doing. But I know how to always try. I know how to listen to my intuition.

I know how to write it all down. I know how to get it all out. I know how to say it out loud. I know how to repeat it until it loses the power to break me.

I know I've been here before. I know I'll be here again. I know I'm stronger than I was the first time.

Growing Numb

It's possible I've gotten a little numb over the past couple of years. It's hard not to. Life can be rough- sometimes it requires all of your strength. It can twist your arm back and make you cry uncle, then laugh as you fall to your knees. I didn't used to be this way. Numb.

I used to weep openly, but I noticed that people began to avoid me. It was as if my heartbreak was contagious and nobody wanted to catch it. So I changed. Life made me.

I became all sass and sarcasm on the outside, all exhaustion and acceptance that life is going to be harder than I anticipated on the inside. Soon things that used to hurt didn't hurt anymore.

I can't tell if this is strength or a slow numbing of the senses. It might be a bit of both. Maybe strength means it takes more to hurt me; means I don't break as easily; or maybe that I understand too much to be offended; that I'm too aware of who I am to take things personally.

Maybe I'm not growing numb.
Maybe I'm just growing up.

Maybe

Maybe what I want and what I need aren't the same thing
Maybe what I want and what is needed from me are not aligned
Maybe I wasn't dreaming big enough
Maybe it was because I was too scared
Maybe I aimed for beauty over substance
Maybe God didn't want me to break in that way
Maybe if I got want I wanted too soon I wouldn't have known to ask
for something better
Maybe I wasn't empathic enough before
Maybe my eyes were a little too closed
Maybe pain was the only way to open them
Maybe I would not have ever learned to comfort myself
Maybe I would have always sought reassurance in other people
Maybe if I never cried I would have never notice the tears of others
Maybe I was too naive
Maybe I needed to mature

Maybe I wasn't brave enough
Maybe I wasn't strong enough
Maybe I wasn't soft enough

Well, now I am.

Rearrange

A Letter from Your Bedroom to You

Desk, dresser, bed, and plastic drawers. I watched you dismantle and haul out all of the furniture you grew up with. Mercilessly you used screwdrivers, hammers, and your bare hands to purge yourself of two decades' worth of memories. At some point you moaned. A sudden moan, like something in you -- something you were trying to suppress -- escaped. You twisted and twisted and twisted that old iron bed frame until it was weak enough to bend to your whim. You folded it up and carried it out like it was an old cardboard box. The weight of it didn't register on your face until after you made it down a flight of stairs and was inching your way up the driveway. Next, you took out the dresser. The desk. The plastic drawers. You poured their contents on the floor and hauled their empty carcasses to the curb like their stench disgusted you. You came back in and laid sweaty on the floor in the midst of the clutter and wept. You wept like you lost everything you ever cared for. You wept like you knew it had to go.

Give Me a Minute

Just for a moment, gather me in your lap and rock me gently. Allow me to bury my face in your shirt as you stroke my hair and place your lips on my forehead.

For just one moment, allow me the luxury of escaping the worries of adulthood, the fears of not being successful; or worse, not living up to my full potential.

Just for one moment, please, allow me to pretend I've already won.

Broken

Look, I'm breaking down here.
I am broken.
I broke.
I broke only a little while ago.
I broke a long time ago.
I broke lifetimes ago.
I sat broken.
I stared at my pieces.
I began to reassemble myself.
I reassembled and reassembled and reassembled.
I did it slowly.
I did it deliberately.
I did it because it had to be done.

It's Time

It's 'bout time somebody told you girl,
he's not coming to save you.
That boy you have been pining over has not been pining over you.
I need you to be okay with this.
I need you to stop waiting for him to put his arm around you
and go out and buy a jacket.
I need you to open up your wings girl,
it's 'bout time you start flying.
It's 'bout time you see what awaits you in the sky.
I'm eager for you to see the beauty that has for too long eluded you.
Loneliness gets easier when you're working towards your vision.
When you start rising you see who rises with you.
That's the difference between a crush and a soul mate.
A crush will stay where he is
a soul mate will rise to meet you.
Water rises to meet its own level
if he doesn't rise
then he is just not on your level
I need you to do you either way.
Keep your heart open girl, and laugh easy.
Love everybody, but don't fall in love with just anybody.
You've only got one heart, spend it wisely.
Take sometime in the mirror to appraise your worth.
Learn to love yourself so you can teach men how to treat you.
Pay no mind to those boys at parties they just want a body,
not necessarily yours,
definitely not you.
They don't see you.
They look at your body and they see away to escape their own hurt.
To them you are a coping mechanism;
you can't change that;
you can't help them.
All you can do is protect yourself.
I hate to say 'because no one else will',
but sometimes it seems that way.

Sometimes it is that way.
Sometimes you are your own biggest advocate,
fight hard for yourself.
Don't make it hard for the right guy later.
Don't make it hard for yourself now.
Above all have faith, have faith that you will be loved in a way you are
worthy of being loved.
In the meantime find what makes you happy and do it.
Do it well.
It takes work to be soft in a world that requires you to be hard.
My soul aches because it is this way.
I want the world to be kind to you.
I want you to be able to love knowing your heart is safe.
I pray you find a man that lets you be soft,
who protects you so you don't always have to be so defensive.
Until then you need to find a safe haven- whether it be a friend, a
notebook, or a quiet room.
Find a place where you can nurture your gentleness.
Find a place that applauds a quiet spirit.

Girl

girl, girl you
you black woman
you
woman
you
black
you
strong
you with arms tucked in tight during this roller coaster of emotions
called your life
you
self-controlled
you
out of control
you
finding the balance that won't leave you rocking quietly in a corner
you
are beautiful. even when it is just you saying it to yourself
you
are kind. even when jealousy makes you want to be mean
you
are tall. standing on the shoulders of women who came before you
you
pray long time. bathing yourself in scripture. finding purity in God's
promises to you.
you
are smart. because you see
you
are scared. because you understand
you
are brave. because you do it anyway
you
girl. girl you
you, got this
and I love you
and we will be strong together

Hope

Dear First Love

Dear First Love,
You are not a poet. But the first time you told me you loved me, I understood what poetry was meant to do. Forget about syntax and clever word play, correct grammar or spell check -- you evoked emotion. You spoke truth and that is by far the hardest part of poetry. I have never said I love you to anyone as boldly as you said it to me. Do you remember that? I was sitting on my bed in the dorms back in Florida. I clutched the phone tightly and whispered, "I'm sorry I can't say it back."

I'm sorry I was too scared to say it back. I think you knew I did, but I should have said it. It doesn't matter now, but it would have mattered then. I have no regrets, though, only lessons learned. You are happy, I am happy, we are happy not together. Yet we are forever tethered by a love once shared. At least I still feel tethered. But it's not in a way that holds me back. It's in a way that sets me free.

It frees me because I remember how much I really did love you. And I remember how scared that made me. I don't want to be scared anymore. The next time someone I love tells me they love me, I want to say it back. I am going to say it back.

Thank you for loving me back then. You taught me more than you know.

No Time for Fear

I think my body is used to rejection. Don't get me wrong -- it hates it. But the sting of "no thank you" does not hurt as much as it used to. I think my body has simply adjusted to the harsh conditions that come with housing me. I profess my feelings often. Because I used to be scared, but now I know I don't have enough time to be afraid. I have so many things I want to do, and so many words I need to say, and I don't know if I'll have enough time to say them all. Many of my wounds have healed, but my scars remind me that I am still running out of time. I am juggling a million things I want to do and I don't have enough hands. So if I think you are awesome -- yes, I will tell you. If I want something in my life -- yes, I will ask for it. If it doesn't work out, which has happened quite a few times, it will be uncomfortable. I will be sad. But at least I will know that I didn't reject myself; I had the courage to say it; I had the courage to ask.

I have too many things to do. I simply do not have time to be afraid.

Bulldog

You're a feisty little bulldog aren't you?
Fragile, but feisty.
Your bark is vicious and you have a bite to match
so people don't think you are delicate.
But I know the truth:
this world scares you.
Love scares you, success scares you, growth scares you
but you carry on anyway.
You're a brave little bulldog, focusing on one step at a time;
constantly moving forward, determined to never give up.

What I Can Do

I can't make somebody love me,
but what I can do is:
write a song,
sing a song,
read a book,
write a book,
create a company,
build an empire,
give advice,
take advice,
listen,
walk away,
say no,
defend myself,
love myself,
be kind to others,
make new friends,
take care of old friends,
I can live with my arms wide open.
I can play sports,
compete,
climb mountains,
run marathons,
feel my heart beating within me.
I can paint,
draw,
sculpt,
create,
I can evoke emotion.
I can design new technology,
be innovative,
be a revolutionary,
be an inspiration,

be a leader.
I can stand up for the defenseless.
I can express my outrage.
I can do something about it.
I can serve those in need.
I can give to the poor.
I can do more than just be angry.
I can let go,
move on,
cry,
and still keep moving.
I can love others even when
I don't feel like it.
I can forgive.
I can be happy.
I can complete myself.
I can be my own better half.
I can make a fool out of myself.
I can go after people out of my league.
I can risk getting rejected.
I can risk falling in love.
I can work on myself.
I can make myself do better.
I can make myself try harder.
I can make myself part of their league.
I can try again.
I can keep my eyes on things above.
I can let love come to me.
I can stop wishing so hard.
I can stop wanting so much.
I can trust God has already heard me.
I can go to sleep now.
I can rest easy.
I can know that everything
that is in my control I am doing to the very best of my abilities

Silence Please

When my entire world went quiet I began to struggle with my words.
When no one was there to listen, did my words still matter?
I stood on stages in front of empty chairs.
I talked to adults who told me to be quiet.
I spoke to children who didn't understand what I was saying.
I was my most devoted audience
and some days I didn't even listen to myself.
I prayed to God daily because He was the only one who had that kind
of time to spare.
I'm starting to think He did that on purpose.
He made it so He was the only one I could talk to.
He said things like "all beautiful you are."
He called me darling.
No one ever calls me darling.
And it didn't stop there, He said all kinds of nice things to me.
I think He kept me in silence to force me into listening.
Maybe He knew I would not have heard Him otherwise.
Eventually, I gave in and stopped fighting the hush that was swept
over my life.
I became still so I could learn what can only be taught when
everything else goes quiet.
At first the silence felt lonely,
but loneliness can be a blessing despite how much it feels like a curse.
After a while, the silence didn't feel like loneliness anymore,
it began to feel like peace.

You Will Be Okay

The inevitable is coming. At some point this, whatever this is, will end. It may end by force or by choice, but either way, all things -- no matter how sweet or how bitter -- end. Knowing that, be it painfully or blissfully aware of that, there are some steps one can take to make it through.

First: one can very simply breathe.

In the good times: take a step back, take a deep breath, and soak in the scenario. Memorize everything beautiful about your world. The sensation of laughing, of reaching out and having someone reach back, of long conversations with someone who gets you, of not having it all figured out and not caring that you don't. Soak that in. During the bitterness of an ending, the memories of a sweet beginning will give you hope for the future. It will be a reminder that loving and losing was not a waste of time.

In the bad times: take a step back, take a deep breath, and evaluate the scenario. Think of every difficult situation as a tool used to strengthen you. What is it that you need to learn? Is it how to let go? How to forgive others? How to forgive yourself? How to ask for more? How to be content with less? How to be brave? How to try? The lessons are infinite and deeply personal. Nobody can tell you what life is trying to teach you. And even if they could, if you are like me, you wouldn't listen. There are many lessons only experience can teach.

Second: one can not-so-simply adjust.

In the good times: gratitude is the main way I've learned to make a good scenario better. The universe rewards gratitude. This is a lesson that I was taught previously, but didn't fully understand until I saw it firsthand. Say thank you, give compliments, give love to everyone who needs it -- and everybody needs it.

In the bad times: gratitude and humility make a difficult scenario bearable. No matter how unfortunate the situation, there are always things to be grateful for. Always. If you don't see any, breathe, take a step back, and look again. Next, be humble -- learn the lesson. I promise you the hard times will not end until you learn the lesson.

That's it. That's all I got. Life is that simple and that complicated. Breathe and adjust. Breathe and adjust. The scenarios are different, but the concepts are always the same. Rest assured that no matter what is going on in your life, you will be okay.

Try Again

Let us try again, to peel off our shells and let someone in.
Even though vulnerability has burned us before.
Let us give it one more try and one more try and one more try,
over and over again.
Not thinking about the last try or the try before that,
only focusing on this try.
This gallant effort to let someone close enough to know us, to touch
us, to change us.
Let us put our luggage of failed love, broken hearts, and traumatic
events into the back seat
and pay attention to the people sitting beside us.
Let us celebrate all who have gone and let them go,
so we can appreciate all who are here and hold them close.

When The Love Is Real

When the love is real you feel it.
You feel like you, not too much and not too little, the perfect amount.
You feel heard, even if you're not understood.
You feel valued.
You feel like you can say and do anything
because you would never say or do anything to hurt the one
-that you finally know without a doubt in your heart-
loves you.
You hurt them anyway, on accident.
Because love always hurts a little bit.
Love always makes mistakes.
Love always apologizes.
Love always hurts when it hurts you.
You can feel the sincerity.
Love puts in the work.
Love comes back, day in and day out.
Love does not leave.
Love stays when it's boring.
Love stays when it's hard.
Love stays as you go through changes.
Love changes with you.
Love tries.
It never stops trying.
It feels like you can finally breath.
It feels like safety.
It feels "I can do this,
with you by my side I can do anything."
It feels like support.
It sounds like a cheerleader,
like an accomplice,
like a voice of reason,
like bail money.
Love feels like, the opposite of empty phrases.
Love doesn't need to say "I love you" because you already know.
But it says it anyway, so there is never any confusion.

This Heart of Mine

Love never leaves you wondering.
Love tells the truth, even when it's hard.
Love feels like a best friend, plus butterflies.
Love feels like a fantasy that was built in reality.
Love feels like, everything that I've been waiting for.

Notes

Notes

Notes

Notes

Notes

Notes

Notes

Notes

www.ingramcontent.com/pod-product-compliance
Lightning Source LLC
Chambersburg PA
CBHW020511030426
42337CB00011B/332